WHY CHRISTIANS SHOULD CARE ABOUT THEIR JEWISH ROOTS

NANCY PETREY

Topical Line Drives, Volume 17

Energion Publications
Gonzalez, FL
2015

ISBN10: 1-63199-103-5
ISBN13: 978-1-63199-103-5

Energion Publications
P. O. Box 841
Gonzalez, FL 32560

energion.com
pubs@energion.com
850-525-3916

DEDICATION

To Janice Horowitz Bell, my Messianic Jewish friend,
with whom I have had priceless spiritual experiences
in ministry, both in the United States and in Israel.
What a loving gift from the God of Israel she has been to me.

ACKNOWLEDGMENTS

First, I want to acknowledge my husband Curtis, who has read the manuscript and given his usual wise advice and insights. He has shown patience and forbearance with my work habits! I love you, Curtis.

Next, I so appreciate my friend, Hannah May, who inspired me to write my first book, *Jewish Roots Journey: Memoirs of a Mizpah*, and who recommended me to her publisher. She has given generously of her time to read and evaluate this manuscript and has greatly helped me with accuracy and scriptural analysis. God bless you, Hannah.

This book would not be in print except for the trust shown me by Henry and Jody Neufeld of Energion Publications. I sincerely thank you.

I am highly indebted to those who prayed for me, my Lovers of Israel e-mail list and others. You know who you are. May Yeshua reward you.

Finally, I acknowledge my blessed Father, my Lord and Savior, Jesus/Yeshua, and His Holy Spirit! It is through His moving through me that this book was accomplished. Thank You, Lord.

INTRODUCTION

Israel and the Jewish people are center stage in our day, and traditional Jewish support in the Church is declining. This book will give convincing proofs from Scripture and church history, answering the question, "Why should Christians care about their Jewish roots?"

It is my prayer that readers, armed with this knowledge, will give fervent support and also pray for the Jewish people and the State of Israel, thereby preparing the way for the return of *Yeshua HaMashiach*, Jesus the Messiah.

CHAPTER ONE
JESUS IS JEWISH

Christian faith is rooted in a Savior, His Holy Land, and His Holy Word. Somehow, the Church has either not realized this or not emphasized that the roots are of Jewish origin. But, should Christians care about this? Why?

First of all, Christians should care about the Jewish roots of the Church, because Jesus Christ, our Savior and Lord, is Jewish. He is the "Anointed One" – the Messiah (Hebrew) and the Christ (Greek). His real Hebrew name is *Yeshua*. The angel said to Joseph, "You shall call His name *Yeshua* (which means *He shall save*), for He will save His people from their sins" (Matthew 1:21). The sentence makes more sense when you know His Hebrew name and what it means.

And the Bible makes more sense when you realize it is a Jewish book, written by Jewish authors, except for Luke. The Old Testament was written entirely in Hebrew with the exception of a tiny bit of Aramaic. Matthew, Mark, Luke, and Acts 1:15-35 are highly Hebraic. Matthew was originally written in Hebrew before being translated into Greek, and the other gospels may have been, too. Add to this the many quotes from the Old Testament in the New Testament, and you get a Bible that is ninety per cent Hebrew![1]

The Jews were the people entrusted with writing down God's Word. The revelation of the one and only true God was given to the Jewish people. The Apostle Paul agonized over the "lostness" of His own people, considering they were chosen by God to know, record, and propagate His truth. He was so upset about it, that He would have traded in his own salvation to see His Jewish brothers saved!

> I could wish myself actually under God's curse and separated from the Messiah, if it would help my brothers, my own flesh and blood, the people of Isra'el! They were made God's

---

1 David Biven & Roy Blizzard Jr., *Understanding the Difficult Words of Jesus*, Revised Ed. (Shippensburg, PA: Destiny Image Publishers, 1994), pp. 4-5

children, the *Sh'khinah*[2] has been with them, the covenants are theirs, likewise the giving of the *Torah*,[3] the Temple service and the promises; the Patriarchs are theirs; and from them, as far as his physical descent is concerned, came the Messiah, who is over all. Praised be *Adonai* forever! Amen!

(Romans 9:3-5, CJB)

God **chose** the Jews, "the least of all peoples," not because of their greatness, but only because He loved them and would keep the covenant He made with "their fathers" (Deuteronomy 7:7-8). This covenant climaxed in God's bringing the Messiah into the world through them! Moses said to the Israelites, "The Lord your God will raise up for you **a Prophet like me from your midst, from your brethren**. Him you shall hear" (Deuteronomy 18:15). The Messiah would be "from your midst, from your brethren," in other words, an Israelite, a Hebrew, a Jew!

The very first words of the New Testament hammer home the Jewish lineage of Jesus: "This is the genealogy of Yeshua the Messiah, son of David, son of Abraham" (Matthew 1:1, CJB). The Wise Men said, "Where is the new-born **King of the Jews**? For we saw His star in the east and have come to worship Him" (Matthew 2:2).

At His birth Yeshua was **reverenced** as "King of the Jews," but at His death, He was **mocked** as "King of the Jews."

Pilate also had a notice written and posted on the stake [cross]; it read,

YESHUA FROM NATZERET
THE KING OF THE JEWS

Many of the Judeans read this notice, because the place where Yeshua was put on the stake was close to the city; and it had been written in **Hebrew**, in Latin, and in Greek (John 19:19-20, CJB).[4]

---

2 "Glory"

3 First five books of the Bible, also called the Pentateuch. *Torah* means "instruction" in Hebrew and in Greek, "law."

4 Biven & Blizzard, pp 12-14 - Notice that Aramaic is not one of the languages translating *Yeshua's* name and title, even though the New International Version denotes Aramaic. Since discovery of the Dead Sea Scrolls in 1947, scholars have

Yeshua was thoroughly Jewish in life and in death, and He remains Jewish as He now sits at the right hand of God the Father, eagerly anticipating coming for His Bride, the Church. He says, "I am the Root and Offspring of **David**, the bright Morning **Star**. And the Spirit and the bride say, 'Come!'" (Revelation 22:16-17, CJB). Every eye will see Him (Revelation 1:7) as the "Star" of redemption will one day split the eastern sky!

The six-pointed **Star of David** is emblazoned today on the flag of the modern Jewish state of Israel. Their flag is actually a *tallit*, the prayer shawl that Jewish men still wear in obedience to God's commandment (Numbers 15:38). Jesus wore a *tallit*. The woman with the issue of blood who touched the hem of Jesus' garment and was healed (Matthew 9:20) was touching the tassel or *tzitzit* on the corner of his *tallit*. It is rare to see any Christian art of *Yeshua* wearing a *tallit*, and yet He must have worn one every day of His life on earth, since he was a Torah-observant Jew.

When Jesus returns, He will not be coming as the Lamb of God to take away the sins of the world, His mission at His first coming, but He will come as the kingly and conquering "Lion of the tribe of **Judah** (root word of **Jews**) ..." (Revelation 5:5). His destination will be Jerusalem, the capital of Israel, "the city of the Great King" (Matthew 5:35). The prophet Zechariah gives an exciting description of this climax of world history, "And in that day His feet will stand on the Mount of Olives, which faces Jerusalem on the east ..." (Zechariah 14:4a).

What more compelling reason can be given for caring about the Jewish roots of our faith than that Jesus was and is Jewish? He is the Jewish Messiah promised to the Jewish people and to the whole world. He was born, lived, died, was raised from the dead in Israel, and He is returning to Israel to reign over all the earth! His bride, the Church, will be by His side.

Christians should rejoice in their identity as the "Bride of Christ." And what bride is not interested in her husband's people, his culture, the home he grew up in, his brothers and sisters? In

---

concluded that although the people were multi-lingual, *Mishnaic* Hebrew was the main spoken language of the Jews in Israel in *Yeshua's* day.

Psalm 45, which is called "The Wedding Psalm," the King Messiah has taken a bride, and he admonishes her to let go of all her past life now that she is joined to Him.

> Listen, daughter! Think, pay attention! Forget your own people and your father's house, and the King will desire your beauty; for He is your Lord, so honor Him.   (Psalm 45:11-12)

As Christians, we should honor our Jewish Messiah by honoring His natural brothers and sisters, the Jews, and by learning more about the Jewish roots of our faith. Historically, the Church seems to have forgotten that Jesus is Jewish. In our church experience He didn't look Jewish, did He?

CHAPTER TWO
JESUS *ANGLICIZED*

Christians cannot understand how the Jews could be so blind as to not recognize their Messiah, but Christians are blind also. They are blind to the Jewishness of their faith. The early Gentile leaders of the church were so blind that they persecuted the Jews who believed in Jesus, forbidding them to keep the biblical feasts, including the Sabbath, and to circumcise their baby boys. Jews were excommunicated from the church for any practices deemed "Jewish." This awful church history will be explored in a later chapter.

Ron Cantor, in his book, *Identity Theft*,[5] shows how *Yeshua's* Jewish identity has been stolen. He has been "anglicized!" Much of the art today portrays Him as more western than Middle Eastern. For instance, in the famous painting of *The Last Supper* by Leonardo da Vinci, we see "thirteen Europeans in Renaissance clothing having a midday meal in an Italian palace ... This work of art is in error in almost every historical detail!" points out Dwight Pryor.[6] The Last Supper was actually a Passover seder, and the correct setting is in the evening, commemorating the night the death angel "passed over" the homes of the Israelites as they were preparing to flee Egypt. In the painting fish and bread are served, but the food Jesus and His disciples had was *matza* (unleavened bread) and a lamb from the Temple sacrifices. In the painting Jesus is seated upright at the center of a long table. However, Jesus and his disciples would have been reclining on the floor on cushions, leaning around a u-shaped table called a triclinium. Jesus, the guest of honor would have been placed in the second position from the

---

5 Ron Cantor, *Identity Theft* (Shippensburg, PA: Destiny Image Publishers, 2013).

6 Dwight Pryor, "The Last Supper – Not Exactly," (Dayton, Ohio: The Center for Judaic Christian Studies, 2014), http://jcstudies.com/articleDetail.cfm?articleId=14

right end. The picture has been robbed of its first century Jewish identity! *Yeshua* has been "anglicized!"

In the Book of Genesis we read the story of Joseph, one of the twelve sons of Jacob (Israel), who was sold into slavery by his jealous brothers and eventually arrived at a position as Prime Minister in Egypt. He became the "Savior" of His family by selling them food during the famine, food he had stored up during the years of plenty in Egypt. Jacob sent his sons from Canaan to Egypt to buy food, and they came face to face with the brother they had sold into slavery. He immediately recognized them, but **they did not recognize Joseph**. He had been living in Egypt a long time and looked Egyptian.

The Pharaoh had given Joseph a Gentile wife, the daughter of a pagan priest. He no longer looked or acted Jewish. To his brothers, he appeared to be a Gentile. The life of Joseph is a beautiful type and shadow of Yeshua who was also rejected by His brothers. Joseph was "received" by the Gentiles as "Savior" from the famine. In the same way, Jesus was "received" by the Gentiles when the gospel was taken to them. (However, in a later chapter, we will see that many Jews did believe in Jesus and formed the early church.)

God has allowed Yeshua to be identified with Gentile Christianity (which does include some Jews). But the time is coming and is already here when the Jewish people will recognize their Jewish Messiah, just as Joseph's brothers finally recognized him. Joseph took the initiative to reveal himself to his brothers, and today Yeshua is lovingly removing the blinders on the Jewish people. The number of Messianic Jews is increasing in Israel and around the world.

I was blessed to attend a Passover Seder in the historic Christ Church in Jerusalem in 2002. Lars Enarson led us. He had prepared a Messianic Haggadah (program booklet), to show Yeshua as the Passover Lamb, the unleavened bread, and in the entire historical account of the great deliverance of the Israelites from Egypt. Lars said upon his completion of writing the *Haggadah* that *Yeshua* whispered to him, "Thank you for restoring my Jewish identity!"

I received another blessing when I heard the testimony of Rabbi Jonathan Bernis[7] on a cruise in 2004. He said before his eyes were opened to see the true identity of Jesus of Nazareth, he thought Jesus was the son of Mr. and Mrs. Christ! Once his eyes were opened, he saw *Yeshua*, who was just as Jewish as he was. Jonathan had been robbed of the truth, because he had only seen an anglicized version of Jesus.

How did we lose the awareness of the Jewishness of Jesus and of Christianity? Blindness set in as the early Church changed from a fully Jewish membership to a Gentile religion.

7 Jewish Voice Ministries, testimony of Jonathan Bernis - http://www.jewish-voice.org/messianic-education/messianic-vision/answering-the-call.html

CHAPTER THREE
THE CHURCH IS JEWISH

The "birthday" of the church has always been considered the Day of Pentecost, described in Acts 2, when the Holy Spirit was poured out on 120 followers of Jesus who had gathered in "the upper room" to pray as Jesus had instructed them. The Hebrew name for this occasion is *Shavuot*, Feast of Weeks, one of the seven yearly "feasts of the Lord" in Leviticus 23. A huge crowd of Jews from far and wide had come to Jerusalem to bring their offerings. The people had counted down seven Sabbaths from the Feast of Firstfruits plus one day. *Shavuot* (Hebrew) denotes seven weeks, and Pentecost (Greek) denotes 50 days (Leviticus 23: 15-16). It was a Feast of Harvest, and after Peter preached, there was definitely a harvest on that day, a harvest of about 3,000 souls (Acts 2:41)! They would all be baptized immediately.

Baptism is a Jewish thing, and there were almost fifty *mikvaot* (baptismal pools) at the foot of the southern stairs of the Temple. I have seen them. The Jews had to cleanse themselves before entering the temple grounds, so the pools had a lot of traffic. And that great number of people who had just been saved needed a lot of water, wouldn't you say? They were immersed, as the word *baptizo* indicates. And every one of them was Jewish. The church had a purely Jewish beginning.

The Jewish character of the early church recorded in Acts and the Epistles has sometimes been misrepresented in English translations of the Bible. For instance, Mary, the mother of Jesus, had the Hebrew name Miriam, but most Bibles use either Maria or Mary. Also, we know Shaul (anglicized *Saul*) as the Apostle Paul and assume his name was changed to Paul after his Damascus road experience (Acts 9). However, his name was not changed. Shaul had preached many years by the time the Bible mentions he was "**also called** Paul" (Acts 13:9), a name that was *in addition to*, not *instead of* Shaul. It was common for Jewish people to have two names, one that related to the culture in which they lived, and a Hebrew name."[8]

More importantly, *Joshua* and *Jesus* are the **same name**. In Hebrew the names are *Yehoshua* and *Yeshua* (shortened form). "While Joshua is seen as Jewish, the Jewish Messiah has been portrayed throughout history as being something other than Jewish."[9] The name of John the Baptist conveys nothing Jewish, but his Hebrew name is *Yohanan*, a distinctly Jewish name.

In his book, *Yeshua, A Guide to the Real Jesus and the Original Church*, Dr. Ron Moseley writes that previous histories of the early Church have left out the Jewish factor and only narrated the history of the later second- and third-century Church after it became mostly Gentile. The Jewish roots of the early Church have been ignored, and historians have not understood that "the early Church was one of the many sects within first-century Judaism, which neither Jesus nor Paul ever tried to leave."[10] Does that surprise you? Even more surprising is that the first fifteen bishops of the church were Jewish.[11] And the history gets better when you know that all these bishops were relatives of *Yeshua*! They served all the way up to the second Jewish revolt, the Bar Kochba Revolt (A.D. 132-135).[12] During the first Jewish revolt against the Romans in A.D. 66-70, the Hebrew Christians fled to the mountains of Pella, located in present-day Jordan, in obedience to the Messiah's instruction in Matthew 24:16. The bishops may have been in exile for a period of time, but the leadership of the church was Jewish until after the second revolt. Then Gentile believers assumed "control of the Church for the first time, and they quickly appointed a man named Mark as Jerusalem's first non-Jewish pastor."[13] The church still kept its Jewish organization, which was like the synagogue.

---

8 Cantor, Chapter 9, "Class is in Session."
9 Ibid.
10 Dr. Ron Moseley, *Yeshua, A Guide to the Real Jesus and the Early Church* (Baltimore: Messianic Jewish Publishers, 1996), p. xviii.
11 Ibid, p. 7, citing Eusebius in his *Ecclesiastical History*, that "faithful Hebrews continued from the time of the apostles until the siege of Jerusalem."
12 Ibid, p. 7.
13 Ibid, p. 8.

During *Yeshua's* three years of ministry on earth He only went to the Jews and sent out His disciples, commanding them to "go rather to the lost sheep of the house of Israel" (Matthew 10:6). But prior to His ascension He commanded His disciples to preach the gospel all over the world (Matthew 28:19), starting from Jerusalem and spreading outward (Acts 1:8). However, they had remained in Jerusalem. The membership of the Church was all Jewish for ten years, until God called Peter to go to Caesarea to the house of Cornelius, a **Gentile** Roman army officer, a "God-fearer." The salvation of Cornelius and his household (Acts 10), a watershed event in church history, marks the beginning of Gentile evangelism.

It is commonly believed that God used Paul to start a new religion, Christianity, in opposition to Judaism whose adherents failed to recognize *Yeshua* as Messiah. Not so. Let us examine the word *Christian*. "It does not come from the Hebrew word for *Anointed One* but from a Greek word, and was not used by the Jerusalem Church at all. *Christian* was first used as a Gentile title for the believers at Antioch some forty to forty-five years into the first century (Acts 11:26). ... It was not a title used by the church, evidently, because we see it only three times in the New Testament and only once by a believer (Acts 11:26, 26:28; I Peter 4:16)." [14]

Paul is known as the Apostle to the Gentiles, but his priority of mission, like *Yeshua's*, was to "**the Jew first**" (Romans 1:16). The Lord sent Ananias to Paul, saying "Go, for he is a chosen vessel of Mine to bear My name before Gentiles, kings, and **the children of Israel**" (Acts 9:15). Notice throughout Acts, Paul is seen going to the synagogue **first** in every town he enters. Once when he preached to the Jews in Corinth and they "opposed him and blasphemed, he shook his garments and said to them, 'Your blood be upon your own heads; I am clean. From now on I will go to the Gentiles'" (Acts 18:6). He left there and went in a home next to the synagogue! He didn't go very far, did he? And only a few verses later we see him coming to Ephesus and entering the **synagogue** to reason with the Jews (vs. 19). So, we can conclude that Paul did not establish a new religion, Christianity, but he

14 Ibid, p. 12-13.

12

preached mostly in synagogues messages from the Hebrew Scriptures (the New Testament had not yet been written) that Yeshua was the promised Messiah to God's covenant people as well as to Gentiles who would believe.

The early church continued to keep the Sabbath, go to the Temple for prayer, and meet house to house every day. Jewish believers continued the annual feasts commanded in the Scripture. This was not a new religion. It was a fulfillment of the covenant faith begun with Abraham and passed down through Isaac, Jacob (Israel), Moses, David, and the prophets.

When Paul reported back to Jerusalem about the great number of Gentiles coming into the church, James and all the elders rejoiced. Then James had a report also. He said, "You see, brother, how many **myriads of Jews** there are who have believed, and they are all zealous for the law" (Acts 21:20). In ancient Greek a myriad was 10,000, so myriads would mean **tens of thousands**! Wow! And these new Jewish believers continued observing the Torah. It was no new religion they embraced, but the fulfillment of the one they already had! This true religion was based on the Torah that God had commanded Moses to write down, as well as the rest of the Old Testament. Their observance was biblical and did not include the man-made "traditions of the elders" that *Yeshua* came against in conflicts with the Pharisees.

The new church, or *kehilah*, as it was called in Hebrew, was definitely Jewish. So, what happened? How did our Jewish roots get cut off? The story is found in the darkest period of church history, in the pages that Christians have cut out of their history books. But these same pages are the ones that the Jewish people have learned only too well.

God must have given Paul a glimpse of these pages, because he set forth an ominous warning to the church in his letter to the Romans. Let us hear the cry of God's heart, trying to avert this pitfall into darkness.

CHAPTER FOUR
WILD BRANCHES

Paul, the consummate Jewish theologian, set forth his theology in his letter to the Romans, and the centerpiece of the letter is Chapters 9, 10, and 11. Maybe you have heard teachings on the first two chapters, but, unless you have already joined the Jewish roots movement, it is doubtful you have heard a sermon on Chapter 11.

Perhaps the favorite verse of evangelists is found in chapter 10: "For if you confess with your mouth the Lord Jesus and believe in your heart that God has raised Him from the dead, you will be saved" (vs. 9). A favorite verse of Christian ministers to establish their calling is in Chapter 11: "For the gifts and the calling of God are irrevocable" (vs. 29). But would it surprise you to learn that the context of these three chapters is all about the Jewish people? It truly is. Paul's message is addressed to the church in Rome, made up mostly of Gentiles. **Verse 1** of each chapter expresses a longing for Israel to be saved (9:1), a prayer that evangelists be sent to the Jewish people (10:1), and a vehement declaration that God has not cast away His people (11:1)! He has reserved a remnant, and it is the job of the Gentiles to "provoke them to jealousy" (Romans 11:11) by the fact that salvation has come to them through the Jews' Messiah! Paul declared himself to be "an apostle to the Gentiles" in order to "provoke to jealousy" his Jewish brothers and "save some of them" (Romans 11:13-14).

Paul points out the benefits of both the **fall** and the **fullness** of the Jews. "Now if their **fall** is riches for the world, how much **more** their **fullness**! ... For if their casting *Yeshua* aside means reconciliation for the world, what will their **accepting him** mean? It will be life from the dead!" (11:12, 15, CJB). That is equivalent to worldwide revival! You can see God's plan to bring redemption to the whole world, even using Israel's rejection of *Yeshua* as part of the plan. "Oh, the depth of the riches both of the wisdom and knowledge of God! How unsearchable are His judgments and His ways past finding out!"(11:33).

14

God Himself blinded the Jews, but only partially, and it is a mystery. He reveals His purpose in doing so:

> For I do not desire, brethren, that you should be ignorant of this mystery, lest you should be wise in your own opinion, that blindness in part has happened to Israel **until the fullness of the Gentiles has come in.** And so **all Israel will be saved,** as it is written: 'The Deliverer will come out of Zion, and He will turn away ungodliness from Jacob; for this is My covenant with them, when I take away their sins. (Romans 11:25-27)

It was the Jewish followers of *Yeshua* who took the gospel to the Gentiles, and in these last days it is now the privilege and blessing for Gentile believers to take the gospel full circle back to Jerusalem. The "**fullness** of the Gentiles" is being reached as more and more Christians understand Paul's admonition to provoke the Jews to jealousy (vs. 11) by their faith in *Yeshua*, "and so," (or "in **this** way") **all Israel will be saved.**" Paul further states God's strategy: "… through the mercy shown **you** [Gentiles], **they** [the Jews] also may obtain mercy" (vs. 31). It is true that most Messianic Jews today were won to *Yeshua* by Gentiles.

One interpretation of "the fullness of the Gentiles" is "full number," but it is not the meaning here. This is the same Greek word, *pleroma*, that Paul uses for the "**fullness**" of the Jews in the same chapter, verse 12, meaning "fulfillment or completion" in opposition to "failure or transgression."

> [The Gentiles'] "fullness" as with Israel is when they both obey and fulfill their respective callings: **Gentile believers mercifully expressing their faith to communicate effectively to Jewish people so they'll be desirous of Yeshua,** and **national Israel** joining the remnant in **accepting Yeshua** and, thus all Israel will be saved, all to the glory of God.[15]

The heart of Paul's message to the Gentiles in the Roman church in chapter 11 is a warning. The Gentiles are not to be prideful that they accepted *Yeshua* and begin to boast against Israel for their **not** accepting Him. Paul uses the picture of an **olive tree**

---

15 Word of Messiah Ministries - http://wordofmessiah.blogspot.com/2010/05/lest-you-be-wise-in-your-own-conceits-i.html#more

to explain the consequences of this boastful attitude. The Gentiles are "wild branches" grafted into a "cultivated olive tree." This tree represents the covenant faith that God gave the Jewish people, beginning with Abraham and his descendants through Isaac and Jacob/Israel. He was looking for a holy people, a set apart people, who would be His own people, and He would be their God. They were chosen to represent Him to the world, and through them He would bless every family of mankind (Genesis 12:1-3). The coming of *Yeshua*, one of their own, would be the realization of that great promise to Abraham. Paul makes his case:

> ... *and if the root is holy, so are the branches, and if* **some** *of the branches were broken off, and you, being a wild olive tree, were grafted in among them, and with them became a partaker of the root and fatness of the olive tree,* **do not boast** *against the branches. But if you do boast, remember that you do not support the root, but* **the root supports you.**" (Romans 11:16b-18)

Notice that Paul said "some" of the branches were broken off, meaning *not all* the Jewish people rejected *Yeshua*, but some stayed connected to the olive tree. The Gentiles should realize that they have benefited from being grafted into a cultivated tree and not brag about it. In other words, don't be like some teenagers who have received so much from their parents but act as if their parents don't exist! They don't honor or even acknowledge their parents.

Paul does not deny that some of the natural branches were broken off to make room for the wild branches, but he warns, "Because of unbelief they were broken off, and you [Gentiles] stand by faith. **Do not be haughty, but fear.** For if God did not spare the natural branches, He may not spare you either" (11:19-21). Tough words! Oh, that the church would heed this admonition!

Here comes the climax and the good news:

> *And they also* [the Jews], *if they do not continue in unbelief, will be grafted in, for God is able to graft them in again. For if you were cut out of the olive tree which is wild by nature, and were grafted contrary to nature into a cultivated olive tree, how much more will these, who are* **natural branches**, *be grafted into their* **own olive tree**?
> (11: 23-24)

The Church should never lose sight of the fact it is a **Jewish** olive tree! These words should inspire Christians to be grateful for their Jewish roots and to guard against a boastful attitude toward the unbelieving Jews.

Ruth was a pagan and idolatrous Moabite, a "wild branch," but she humbly learned from Naomi, a "natural branch." Ruth was grafted into the Jewish olive tree when she became the wife of Boaz, her kinsman-redeemer – a type of Messiah – and she became the great-grandmother of King David. She vowed, "Wherever you go I will go …. Your people shall be my people, and your God, my God" (Ruth 1:16). In relation to her Jewish mother-in-law, Ruth was the epitome of caring.

Likewise, the Ephesian believers were wild branches. Paul said, "Therefore, remember your former state: you Gentiles by birth … had no Messiah. You were estranged from the national life of Israel. You were foreigners to the covenants embodying God's promise. You were in this world without hope and without God" (Ephesians 2:11-12 CJB). But by the blood of Christ, Gentiles and Jews became "one new man" and the wall of separation was broken down (Ephesians 2:13-15).

Where is the gratitude that Gentile believers should have for their Jewish heritage? Unfortunately, in total disregard of Paul's warnings, as early as the second century the Church began to separate from its Jewish roots and began to actively persecute the Jews. Gentile leaders tried to take over the olive tree and get rid of the natural branches! They adopted "**replacement theology**," claiming that the Church was the "new Israel," who inherited all the blessings of God, leaving the Jews with the curses! How did this happen?

17

CHAPTER FIVE
NOT CARING LED TO THE HOLOCAUST

So far we have seen that Christians should care about their Jewish roots because Jesus/*Yeshua* is Jewish. Anglicizing or westernizing Him is stealing His identity and giving an unscriptural picture of Him. Christians should care that the Bible was written by Jews, and the disciples and early Church were all Jews. They should recognize that Gentile believers were wild branches grafted into a cultivated Jewish olive tree and should be thankful for their Jewish roots which support and nourish them. We can conclude from all this that it is the right thing and the "Christian" thing to care about the Jewish roots of the Church. But what about caring for Jewish **people** and caring for the Jewish State of **Israel**? It is a sober fact that not caring for their Jewish roots, the largely Gentile Church got off into much theological error which eventually fueled the fires of the Holocaust.

I first began to care when I attended a conference, "Israel in Prophecy," at Christ for the Nations Institute in Dallas, Texas, the summer of 1995. This was fresh revelation to me, and I furiously made notes. After three days, I had 41 pages of notes! I summarized what I had learned in 38 outstanding statements. The one which most strongly impacted me was: "Martin Luther wrote *Concerning the Jews and Their Lies*. It became official Nazi propaganda (published by Goebbels in 1936). Only in the 1980s did some Lutheran churches disown this book."[16] I tell all about this life-changing conference in my book, *Jewish Roots Journey: Memoirs of a Mizpah*.[17]

Hear the words of Martin Luther (1483-1546): "What shall we do with this damned, rejected race of Jews? First, their syn-

---

16 See http://en.wikipedia.org/wiki/On_the_Jews_and_Their_Lies (last accessed 5/19/15.

17 Nancy Petrey, *Jewish Roots Journey, Memoirs of a Mizpah* (Gonzalez, Florida: Energion Publications, 2012).

agogues should be set on fire. ... Secondly, their homes should likewise be broken down and destroyed. ...We ought to drive the rascally lazy bones out of our system. ... Therefore away with them. ... so that you and we may all be free of this insufferable devilish burden – the Jews."[18]

I was stunned, but little did I realize at the time that it was only "the tip of the iceberg." The man known to us as "the father of the Reformation" and the composer of the well-loved hymn, *A Mighty Fortress is Our God*, in this booklet had "injected a dangerous virus into the emerging Protestant churches, a virus that had already been at work hundreds of years in the Roman Catholic Church."[19]

For instance, St. John Chrysostom (344-407), Bishop of the Church at Antioch, a great orator, and one of the greatest of the "early Church Fathers," said, "The synagogue is worse than a brothel ... it is the Temple of demons ... and the cavern of devils ... a place of meeting for the assassins of Christ. ... As for me, I hate the synagogue. ... I hate the Jews for the same reason."[20] Of all the Church fathers, Chrysostom spoke most viciously against the Jews.

How could Luther, Chrysostom, and other leading churchmen spew such Jew-hatred? Richard Booker answers the question with his overview of the tragic history of Christian anti-Semitism in his booklet, "How the Cross Became a Sword."[21] He says that the two basic contributing factors to this tragedy were the separation of Christianity from its Jewish roots followed by the Gentile acceptance and paganization of Christianity. After two Jewish revolts of A.D. 70 and A.D. 135, followers of Jesus were considered traitors and heretics by the larger Jewish community, having followed *Yeshua's* warning to flee from Jerusalem (Matthew 24:16). The center of Christianity moved to Gentile cities. Rabbinical Judaism developed, and Christianity was no longer perceived as a sect of Judaism.

---

18 Martin Luther, *Concerning the Jews and Their Lies* (Reprinted in Talmage, Disputation and Dialogue, pp. 34-36).
19 Petrey, p. 37.
20 *The Roots of Christian Anti-Semitism* (New York: Liberty Press, 1981), p. 27.
21 Richard Booker, "How the Cross Became a Sword" (The Woodlands, Texas: Sounds of the Trumpet, 1994).

The paganization of Christianity took root when a Greek world view was taught in the first seminaries in Alexandria, Egypt. Jesus had said, "Go into the world and make disciples" (Matthew 28:19), but the Gentile church adopted the philosophy of Plato and retreated to the monastery. Plato taught dualism, a belief that the physical or material world was bad, and we should be otherworldly minded and seek escape from this world.[22] The Church glorified celibacy, deeming marriage as an inferior lifestyle. Life was divided into sacred and secular, and creeds replaced deeds. The Church denied the literal realm of the kingdom of God and accepted only the spiritual realm.

Ignoring the original Hebraic understanding of Scripture, most of the early Church Fathers were very anti-Semitic. Tertullian (160-220) blamed the entire Jewish race for the death of Jesus. Origen (185-253) may have been the most responsible one for the early growth of anti-Semitism in the Church."[23] He accused the Jews of plotting to kill Christians. Eusebius (263-339), a student of Origen, wrote the first three centuries of church history and taught that the Church was the "true Israel of God" that had **replaced** literal Israel in God's covenants.

The writings of Augustine (354-430) became the theological textbook for the Church. He used Origen's **allegorical** method of interpreting Scripture. This Greek method denies the **literal** meaning of the text and looks for hidden meanings, **spiritualizing** the relationship between the Church and the Jews concerning the end times and the kingdom of God. The Scriptures that promise judgment and curses on Israel are interpreted literally, but promised blessings are applied spiritually to the Church! Booker said, "Augustine wrote that the Jews deserved death, but instead, they were destined to wander the earth as a witness to their punishment and the victory of the Church over the synagogue. The greater their humiliation, the greater the triumph of the Church. Thank God that the Catholic Church has finally acknowledged the error

---

22 Ibid, p. 11.
23 Stan Telchin, *Abandoned*, (Grand Rapids: Chosen Books, 1997), p. 54.

of this teaching and formally refuted much of it."[24] Unfortunately, replacement theology is still taught and believed in many churches today. **Many Christians don't care about the nation of Israel or their Jewish roots, since they believe the Church has replaced Israel.**

The outcome of these theological underpinnings is shocking. Anti-Semitic atrocities resulted in the bloody path of the Crusades, the Inquisition, the pogroms, and the Holocaust. A good starting point for this litany of woes befalling the Jewish people at the hands of the Church is Emperor Constantine's Council of Nicea in A.D. 325. His purpose was to unify the Roman Empire by converting it to the Christian religion. Under the influence of his advisor, Eusebius, Constantine severed the Jewish roots of the Church permanently. He refused the biblical dating for the observance of Christ's death, burial, and resurrection shown in the Feasts of Passover, Unleavened Bread, and Firstfruits (Leviticus 23), and replaced it with his own date for Easter. Constantine's hatred of the Jews was obvious:

> It seems to everyone a most unworthy thing that we should follow the customs of the Jews in the celebration of this most holy solemnity, who, polluted wretches! having stained their hands with a nefarious crime, are justly blinded in their minds. It is fit, therefore, that rejecting the practice of this people, we should perpetuate to all future ages the celebration of this rite, in a more legitimate order, which we have kept from the first day of our "Lord's" passion even to the present times. Let us then have nothing in common with the most hostile rabble of the Jews.[25]

Jewish Christians could no longer observe Passover, circumcision, nor Sabbath worship under threat of excommunication. The Roman pagan calendar replaced the Jewish (biblical) calendar, and Jesus' resurrection would now be celebrated on Easter, the spring festival when the pagans worshiped Ishtar. Good Friday became

---

24 Booker, p. 17.
25 Babylon Forsaken Ministries, "The Truth About Easter," http://www.babylonforsaken.com/easter.html

the date of Jesus' crucifixion instead of Passover. Jesus' birthday was fixed on December 25, the birthday of the Sun, the high god of the Romans. The biblical Sabbath was replaced with Sunday, the day of weekly Sun god worship. Jewish Christians had to formally renounce their Jewishness and convert to the Gentile brand of Christianity. Pagans flooded into the Church, but they never had a personal relationship with Jesus as Lord and Savior.

Although not biblical, it seems God has allowed this Gentile calendar for a season, until the "fullness of the Gentiles has come in" (Romans 11:25). Now His Spirit is moving in the Church, and Christians are reconnecting with their Jewish roots, learning their history and repenting of past atrocities against the Jews.

There is not a better book on this subject than *Our Hands Are Stained With Blood, The Tragic Story of the "Church" and the Jewish People* by Dr. Michael Brown.[26] It is truly a classic. The book is well-documented, easy to read, and emotionally engaging. Brown tells of horrendous lies perpetrated against the Jews. Many were blamed for the Black Death that ravaged Europe in 1348-1349, wiping out a third of the population. It was believed that the Jews were the culprits, because the plague bypassed them. No one realized that because the Jews kept the food laws of the Torah, they survived.

"Desecrating the host" was another lie. In 1215, the Fourth Lateran Council accepted the doctrine of transubstantiation, a belief that the wafer (host) used at the Mass was miraculously transformed into the body of Jesus. The Church tortured and murdered thousands of Jews, charging them with stealing the host to crucify the body of Jesus again. In 1243, the entire Jewish community in Berlin was burned alive for allegedly "desecrating the host."

The most believed lie through the ages was the charge of ritual murder: This was the claim that the Jews would kidnap a Christian child before Easter, torture and crucify him, drink his blood, and save some later for making Passover matzah! This blood libel

---

26 Dr. Michael Brown, *Our Hands Are Stained With Blood, The Tragic Story of the "Church" and the Jewish People* (Shippensburg, PA, Destiny Image Publishers, 1992).

resulted in the deaths of tens of thousands of Jews at the hands of angry "Christians."

Holy Crusades for Christ, military expeditions, were launched by the Church in the eleventh, twelfth, and thirteenth centuries to emancipate the Holy Land from the Muslims. Crusader armies marched through Europe and the Middle East and on the way committed atrocities against both Jews and Muslims. They captured Jerusalem in 1099. The Jews had taken refuge in the chief synagogue, but the Crusaders burned it down while circling the synagogue on their horses, singing *Christ, We Adore Thee*, crosses held high! All this was considered fitting punishment for the Jews, the "murderers of Christ." [27] After the Crusades came the Inquisitions.

The Inquisition of the Roman Catholic Church was instituted to discover and punish heresy among **Christians** in 1233, but by 1288, the first mass burning of **Jews** on the stake took place in France. In 1481, the Inquisition started in Spain. Tens of thousands of Jews were forced to be baptized. These new Christians, known as *Conversos*, or *Marranos* or *Anusim*, were watched closely to see if they were practicing Judaism secretly. If caught, they were tortured and burned and their property confiscated by the Inquisition Court. **Practicing Jews** met the same fate. Until 1820, over 350,000 Jews suffered punishment.[28]

After the Inquisition came the **pogroms** of Russia. From 1881 to 1902, pogroms ("destruction" – looting, murder, and rape) were carried out against Jews. The Church endorsed some of these attacks, and authorities stood by and watched. The popular movie, *Fiddler on the Roof*, depicts Jewish life in that context. During this time *The Protocols of the Learned Elders of Zion* was published in 1905. This was a supposed conversation between Jewish leaders on how they were to take over the world. This booklet has proven

---

27 Brown, pp. 92-94.
28 Clarence H. Wagner, *Where Was Love & Mercy? Christian Anti-Semitism: Overcoming the Curse* (Bridges for Peace: Jerusalem, Israel, 2004 – out of print), p. 20.

over and over again to be false, but it is still being printed and distributed around the world.[29] It is a best-seller in the Arab world.

All these anti-Semitic lies and atrocities against the Jews down through history confirm that the Church indeed has blood on her hands! Jewish people during the Holocaust believed that Hitler and the Nazis represented Christianity. Where were the true Christians during the Holocaust? Some risked their lives to help the Jews, but the great majority assisted the Nazis in murdering them. The crematoriums could mass murder 25,000 human beings every day. Professor Eliezer Berkovits, a leading Jewish thinker, said:

> After nineteen centuries of Christianity, the extermination of six million Jews, among them one-and-a-half million children, carried out in cold blood in the very heart of Christian Europe, encouraged by the criminal silence of virtually all Christendom, including that of an infallible Holy Father in Rome, was the natural culmination of this bankruptcy. A straight line leads from the first act of oppression against the Jews and Judaism in the fourth century to the holocaust in the twentieth.[30]

These few facts prove my case that Christians not caring about their Jewish roots led to the Holocaust. But what lessons did the Church learn from this atrocity that grew out of replacement theology, a false interpretation of Scripture?

---

29 Ibid, p. 24.
30 Eliezer Berkovits, "Judaism in the Post-Christian Era," reprinted in Talmage, *Disputation and Dialogue*, p. 287.

CHAPTER SIX
ANTI-SEMITISM IN DISGUISE

Today, anti-Semitism has a new target, the State of Israel. This age-old hatred of Jews is now disguised as anti-Zionism and Christian Palestinianism. Evidently, many Christians have not learned the lesson of the Holocaust.

The term "Zionism" was coined in 1890 by Nathan Birnbaum. It means the national movement for the return of the Jewish people to their homeland and the resumption of Jewish sovereignty in the Land of Israel.[31] My friend, Janice Bell, and I attended a *Yom Kippur* service at a Jerusalem synagogue in 2003 and met Dr. Shimon Samuels, the Director for International Relations for the Simon Wiesenthal Center, which confronts anti-Semitism and teaches the lessons of the Holocaust. I relate our conversation in my book.[32] He told us that at the United Nations Conference on Racism in Durban, South Africa in 2001,[33] the participants called for the expulsion of Israel, accusing them of racism in their treatment of the Palestinians. They equated *Zionism* with *racism*. As for racism, Dr. Martin Luther King, Jr. understands that better than anyone, and he was an outspoken supporter of Israel and their right to the Land that God has given them. King said, "When people criticize Zionists, they mean Jews. You're talking anti-Semitism."[34]

At the U.N. conference, copies of *The Protocols of the Learned Elders of Zion* were on sale, and protesters chanted, "Zionism is racism, Israel is apartheid," and "You have Palestinian blood on your hands." The American and Israeli delegations withdrew. Dr. Samuels said that 6,000 Christians came and stood with Israel! What refreshing news. He added, **"Evangelical Christians are the best friends Israel has!"** These Christians obviously cared about

---

31 http://www.jewishvirtuallibrary.org/jsource/Zionism/zionism.html
32 Petrey, p. 141.
33 http://www.midstreamthf.com/200111/feature.html
34 http://www.jewishvirtuallibrary.org/jsource/History/MLKandIsrael.html

their Jewish roots. Unfortunately, since that time more and more evangelical Christians are turning against the Jewish State. More about that later. What about mainline churches?

In June 2014, the General Assembly of the Presbyterian Church (USA) voted 310-303 to divest from three American companies whom they said profit from Israel's *occupation* of Palestinians in the West Bank, "destroying homes and lives."[35] This Presbyterian Church has joined the **BDS** movement – **boycott, divest, sanctions** – against Israel, a campaign which has spread all over the world, into the churches and especially on college and university campuses. It is not about human rights. It is about hating Jews and is "rooted in anti-Semitism and fueled by ignorance."[36] The churches may disavow hating Jews, but their opposition to the Jewish State is anti-Semitism in disguise, influenced by replacement theology.

Another example of anti-Zionism can be found in my own childhood church, the United Methodist Church (not its individual members, many of whom love and support Israel and the Jewish people). The UMC General Conference in 2004 adopted a resolution, "Opposition to Israeli Settlements in Palestinian Land."[37] This document is a classic example of the BDS movement. My friend, Hannah May, was very disturbed when she stumbled upon this Resolution and read the text. She wrote in her book, *Operation Olive Branch, A Collection of Mysteries Uncovered by a Spiritual Sleuth*, "It seemed as though, unbelievably, they were asking the Israelis, not only to stop settling, but to give back land that I believed the Bible was saying belonged to Israel, and to which they had modern-day ownership…. The Bible clearly shows God's

35 http://www.timesofisrael.com/we-cannot-profit-from-the-destruction-of-homes-and-lives-presbyterians-say/
36 http://www.israelnationalnews.com/Articles/Article.aspx/14358#.VDlYEvl-dVsY
37 http://www.umc.org/what-we-believe/opposition-to-israeli-settle-ments-in-palestinian-land

everlasting and eternal covenant with Israel for the land" (Psalm 105:6-15).[38]

Hannah's sleuthing, fortunately, led to a happier discovery about the UMC. Methodism's founders, John and Charles Wesley, were ardent Zionists! Some of Charles Wesley's hymns were Zionist hymns. Hannah wrote, "They believed that the Jewish people were to return in a physical sense to their homeland, receive the Jewish Messiah (Jesus) and would be a light to the nations!"[39] Yes, Zionism is God's plan.

Since the rebirth of Israel in 1948, Palestine is no longer the correct designation for the **Land of Israel**. And it wasn't in Jesus' day either, even though the maps in the back of most Bibles are titled *Palestine*. The land was called Israel when the wise men came to Bethlehem (Matthew 2:20, 21). There was no Palestine then. It was not until A.D. 135, after the Bar Kochba Revolt, that the Roman Emperor Hadrian renamed the land Syria Palaestina, which was later anglicized to Palestine.

The Palestinians today have their own maps which do not show Israel at all! The "two-state solution" is not what they want. They want **all the land**! They put out propaganda that the Jews stole the land from them. Our friend, Lars Enarson, who lives in Israel and is founder of *The Watchman International*, a ministry of worldwide prayer and Bible teaching, disproves this:

> 3. The San Remo Conference in 1920, where both Jewish and Arabic leaders and organizations were represented, gathered on behalf of the League of Nations to decide the future of the Ottoman Empire after World War I. This conference "recognized the historic rights of the Jewish people to reconstitute their national home" in Palestine. [15] Notice carefully the words used. The conference did not create any new right. They recognized an already existing historic right! The San Remo Declaration, together with Article 22 of the Covenant of the League of Nations and Article 80 in the Charter of the United Nations, are still applicable today and binding under

38 Hannah May, *Operation Olive Branch: A Collection of Mysteries Uncovered by a Spiritual Sleuth* (Gonzalez, FL: Energion Publications, 2011), pp. 118, 119.
39 Ibid, p. 194.

International Law. **Forcing Israel to go back to 1967 lines and dividing Jerusalem is therefore a serious breach of International Law.** ...

5. "One can scour thousands of Arab books and newspapers written before 1964 and you will find no mention of an Arab/Muslim Palestinian state, or a reference to Arabs as Palestinians."[17] ...

7. The Jewish people did not take over the land from the Arabs (or Palestinians) but from the Turks. **The Arabs did not own it, the Turks did.**[40]

The age-old Arab-Israeli conflict, which began in the Ishmael-Isaac conflict and continued in the Esau-Jacob conflict (Genesis 15-17, 21, 25, 27), is still bearing bitter fruit in the Holy Land today. God made generous provision for the Arabs, descendants of Ishmael and Esau, but His covenant was with Abraham, Isaac, and Jacob/ Israel. Moreover, He identified Himself to Moses as the **God of Abraham, Isaac, and Jacob, saying "This is My name forever, and this is My memorial to all generations"** (Exodus 3:15). Their descendants, the Jews, were promised the Holy Land, which was first defined to Abraham as the land from the Nile River to the Euphrates River (Genesis 15:18).

In his book, *When Day and Night Cease*,[41] Ramon Bennett gives a prophetic study of world events and how prophecy concerning Israel affects the nations, the Church, and the individual. The title alludes to God's guarantee that Israel will exist as long as the sun, moon and stars exist! (Jeremiah 31:35-36). Bennett explains that the Muslim struggle for an Islamic state is not a territorial dispute, because the 22 Arab nations have over **eight million** square miles of land, and Israel has only **eight thousand,** six hundred thirty square miles. God has deeded the land to Israel, a fact which the world rejects, because they reject the authority of God's Word.

---

40 http://thewatchman.org/en/palestine-what-is-the-truth/
41 Ramon Bennett, *When Day and Night Cease* (Citrus Heights, California: Shekinah Books, 1996).

Muslims believe that Judaism and Christianity are superseded by Islam, and the Koran is the final revelation of God with Muhammad as His prophet. To their great dismay, in 1948, Israel was recreated in the center of the Islamic heartland, proving the Bible to be true and the Koran false! They could not accept that. The Koran demands that jihad be waged until Israel is wiped out. All peace plans have and will fail because of misunderstanding the **real reason** for the conflict – **Islam.**[42] Besides Bennett's book, Richard Booker's booklet, "Islam, Christianity and Israel," is a valuable resource for understanding Islam.[43]

The new-born State of Israel was attacked the next day after they became a nation, May 14, 1948, by **seven** large Arab armies, and it is interesting to note that Joshua's conquest of Canaan also involved "**seven** nations greater and mightier than you" (Deuteronomy 7:1). Israel miraculously defeated their enemies, and Jews fleeing from the surrounding hostile Arab countries were absorbed into the fledgling State. The numbers of Arab refugees and Jewish refugees from the wars of 1948-1973 were roughly the same. "Of the 850,000 Jewish refugees from ten Arab nations, not a one has received a penny in return for the inestimable properties left behind."[44] Western media decries only the **Arab** refugees, but the **Jewish** refugees' losses in northern African countries alone reached at least seven billion dollars![45] The Arabs remaining in Israel were offered citizenship, and today 1.6 million Israeli-Arabs are prospering. On the contrary, the rich Arab nations did not absorb their own refugees but left them on the borders of the Land of Israel, languishing in camps, a breeding ground for terror.

On July 8, 2014, the Hamas terrorists, in unrelenting rocket attacks, instigated a 50-day war in Gaza, having plotted to infiltrate Israel via 32 sophisticated tunnels and massacre unsuspecting Israelis. The plot was discovered and thwarted by the Israel De-

---

42 Ibid, pp. 192-194
43 Richard Booker, *Islam, Christianity and Israel* (The Woodlands, Texas: Sounds of the Trumpet, 1994).
44 Bennett, p. 211.
45 Ibid, p. 212.

fense Force (IDF) during Operation Protective Edge. All the while Hamas was pummeling Israel with thousands of rockets, Israel was sending 959 tons of medicine and medical supplies on 5,359 trucks into Gaza to help their enemies! [46] Jihadists used their own people as human shields and fired rockets from their schools, hospitals, and homes. In stark contrast, the IDF sent advance warnings to Gaza citizens before surgical airstrikes through leaflets, text messages, and the "roof-knocking method."[47] The IDF is the most humane army in the world, but in spite of their extraordinary efforts to avoid civilian casualties, they are being accused of war crimes!

Hamas, Hezbollah, other terrorist groups, and now ISIS obviously want to destroy Israel, but there is a group more insidious in its approach. They seem blind to the compassionate actions of the Israeli government toward the Palestinians. These are **Christian Palestinianists**.

> They push Palestinian propaganda into the very heart of **evangelicalism**. This is very different from the left wing views of Palestinian advocates who worked the Catholic and mainline churches (United Methodist, Episcopalian, Presbyterian, Lutheran) for decades. ... They disseminate the so-called **Palestinian Narrative (short version: everything's Israel's fault)** specifically to the Evangelical community in America. ... Famous and influential seminaries like Fuller are soaked in anti-Israel activism. ... The Southern Baptist Convention, long a friend to Israel, is now showing signs of takeover. ... Dr. Russell Moore, president of the SBC's Ethics & Religious Liberty Commission ... maintains that the **church**, not any current geo-political entity, is the **"new Israel," the inheritor of all Israel's covenant promises.**[48]

In this statement you can hear echoes of the early Church Fathers' replacement theology!

46 http://www.jpost.com/Operation-Protective-Edge/50-days-of-Israels-Gaza-operation-Protective-Edge-by-the-numbers-372574
47 BreakingIsraelNews.com - Top US General: Israel Went Through "Extraordinary Lengths" to Save Lives in Gaza, November 7, 2014.
48 http://www.breakingisraelnews.com/20195/hating-jews-absolutely-necessary/#vBMgF8VKAgD1Bud1.97

Their major gathering is Christ at the Checkpoint biennial conferences since 2010, at Bethlehem Bible College. One point of their Manifesto states: "Any exclusive claim to land of the Bible in the name of God is not in line with the teaching of Scripture."[49] This is an anti-Zionist position and refutes the Abrahamic covenant. Although they purport to work for peace, justice, and reconciliation,

> CATC organizers do not want to hear from those Israeli voices that have been victimized by Palestinian terrorism or able to expose the Palestinian nationalist agenda. In late 2010, Israeli tour guide Kay Wilson and her visiting Christian friend, Kristine Luken, were attacked by Palestinian terrorists outside Jerusalem. Luken was killed and Wilson suffered severe injuries. Wilson approached one of the CATC speakers about speaking at the 2012 convocation, but was told that her story was "not what the Lord wants" .... Wilson then expressed dismay about "how any Israeli.... Messianic believer, could justify participating in **a conference that has chosen to associate itself with theologians advocating Replacement Theology and Palestinian officials with clear ties to recognized terrorist organizations** ... For any self-respecting person, and especially for Israelis such as myself, **the endorsement of terror by association, at a Christian conference, is obscene.**[50]

The anti-Israel narrative of "Christ at the Checkpoint" is now being shared at major Christian conferences in the United States.[51] For many years Palestinian Christians such as Naim Ateek, Anglican priest and founder of Palestinian Liberation Theology[52], have traveled the country telling American Christians how their "brothers and sisters in Christ" are being oppressed by Israel's Jews.[53]

49 http://www.christatthecheckpoint.com/index.php/about-us/manifesto
50 http://www.gatestoneinstitute.org/4230/christ-at-the-checkpoint
51 David Brog, "The End of Evangelical Support for Israel?" – Middle East Quarterly, Spring 2014, http://www.meforum.org/3769/israel-evangelical-support
52 Based on social justice as seen through the eyes of the poor. Detractors call it "Christianized Marxism." http://en.wikipedia.org/wiki/Liberation_theology#cite_note-3
53 Brog, ibid.

But they don't tell about the oppression coming from **Palestinian** leaders. The exodus of Christian Arabs from Bethlehem is because of **Palestinian, not Jewish** oppression.[54] Also, they decry the checkpoints and the security fence (or wall), but these are measures **forced** on Israel in order to keep out suicide bombers and stop sniper fire on vehicles. These measures benefit both Palestinians and Jews.[55]

I had an experience back in 1997 concerning a UMC missionary, Alex Awad, who is a Palestinian pastor and Dean of Students at Bethlehem Bible College. I read in the newspaper about his speaking tour of UM churches in Mississippi. Due to my efforts, he was prevented from speaking on American Family Radio. Fast forward to the 2014 war in Gaza. Awad said, "… **we side with our Palestinian brothers and sisters, even the Muslims**, because we know they are the ones under occupation, they are the ones who are under oppression, and we see that because it is very obvious for people who live here **who** is actually violating the other human rights."[56] Awad seemed oblivious to the fact that Israel was fighting a defensive war!

Films, conferences and tours of Israel are vehicles for Palestinianism. In 2010, three major film documentaries came out, attacking Christian support for Israel. *Little Town of Bethlehem*, funded and produced by Mart Green, was a "masterpiece of deception."[57] A major conference for **young** evangelical leaders called *Catalyst* is pushing the one-sided Palestinian narrative. "Young evangelical stars are bonding on trips to Israel and the Palestinian Authority and are returning to push their fellow evangelicals away from the Jewish state."[58]

---

54 Algemeiner Journal is New York-based Jewish newspaper - http://www.bethlehemfreedom.com/news/article/Baptist-church-in-Bethlehem-declared-illegitimate
55 http://www.jewishvirtuallibrary.org/jsource/Peace/fence.html
56 http://www.christianpost.com/news/palestinian-christian-western-christians-dont-understand-gaza-israeli-conflict-123272/
57 Brog, ibid.
58 Ibid.

The good news is that the pro-Israel side is still far ahead in winning the hearts of American evangelicals. John Hagee's ministry, *Christians United for Israel*, has over 1.6 million members, chapters on more than 120 college campuses, and sponsors 35 pro-Israel events across the country every month.[59] Anti-Israel Christians do not come close to matching this influence. And another hopeful report comes from Robert Stearns, head of *Eagles' Wings*, a global movement of churches, leaders, and ministries. He says that there is "growing, organized support for Israel from new corners of our planet," and "the global center for evangelical Christianity is no longer North America."[60]

Being pro-Israel does not mean being anti-Palestinian. There are many Christian Arabs who love and support Israel and appreciate their Jewish roots. Some of these have come from a Muslim background, and they are often in danger. They need our prayers and our love. We cannot lessen our support for Israel's biblical claim to the Land, but our Christian Zionism must not cancel out our love for the Palestinians, who often are victims of their religion and their leaders.

Yes, anti-Zionism and Palestinianism are nothing more than anti-Semitism cleverly disguised. We should always remember God's eternal promise to Abraham and his descendants, the Jews:

> *I will bless those who bless you, and I will curse him who curses you; and in you all the families of the earth shall be blessed.* (Genesis 12:1-3)

---

59 Ibid.
60 http://www.jpost.com/Christian-News/Evangelical-support-for-Israel-Look-to-the-east-379026

Chapter Seven
CARING ILLUMINATES SCRIPTURE

Once Christians acknowledge and embrace their Jewish roots, they find Scripture is greatly illuminated for them. They begin to see that Christianity is Jewish![61] *Yeshua* said, "Salvation is of the Jews" (John 4:22). They learn that the "Feasts of the Lord" (Leviticus 23) form God's Calendar of Redemption and see the fulfillment, past and future, of all seven feasts in the first and second comings of the Messiah. Christians will realize that God has preserved the Jewish people for the first coming and will, likewise, preserve them for the second coming. Because of their kinship with the Jews, they will see the need to love and support them and their nation of Israel in these last days. Christians will see prophecy being fulfilled right before their eyes! They will also learn of the types and shadows of the Jewish Messiah in the stories of the patriarchs, especially Isaac and Joseph, in the life of Moses and the Tabernacle, and in the nation of Israel in its suffering and victories.

So many Christians avoid the Old Testament, because they think it is hard to understand, and the New Testament is really all they need to understand their salvation and follow Jesus. But Paul said, "**All Scripture** is given by inspiration of God, and is profitable for doctrine, for reproof, for correction, for instruction in righteousness, that the man of God may be complete, thoroughly equipped for every good work" (II Timothy 3:16-17). Paul was referring to the Old Testament, because the **New Testament** had not yet been written! This is the Scripture the Jews use today, but they call it the *Tanakh*, an acronym (TNK) for **T**orah (Law) – **N**eviim (Prophets) – **K**etuvim (Writings). Their books are arranged differently from our Old Testament, but they are the same.

Yeshua validated this three-fold division of Scripture, when He said, "These are the words I spoke to you while I was still with you,

---

61 Edith Shaeffer, *Christianity is Jewish* (Wheaton: Tyndale House Publishers, Inc., 1975 by L'Abri Fellowship, Huemoz, Switzerland.

that all things must be fulfilled which were written in the **Law of Moses** and **the Prophets** and **the Psalms** concerning Me" (Luke 24:44). The Psalms head the division called Writings. **This was the Bible that *Yeshua* and His Apostles used, and every book is about Him!** The popular saying is that Jesus in the Old Testament is **concealed** but in the New Testament **revealed**. We can learn so much about Him by knowing the Jewish/Hebrew context of the Scripture. For instance, **He identifies with His Jewish brothers in the end time judgment of the nations**: "…inasmuch as you did it to one of the least of these **My brethren**, you did it to Me" (Matthew 25:40). The nations who curse Israel will "go away into everlasting punishment," but the nations who bless Israel will go "into eternal life" (Matthew 25: 45-46). This is in accord with God's promise to Abraham (Genesis 12:3). Ramon Bennett says that God declares Abram "to be essentially connected with the prosperity and the misfortune of all who come in contact with him."[62]

Gentiles are included as His "brethren," if we do God's will (Matthew 12:50). In these last days God is bringing Jewish and Gentile believers together. We have been grafted into a Jewish olive tree, and we will soon be more aware of it when we are persecuted together. It may take this for *Yeshua's* prayer to be answered that we be "one" (John 17:11).

God declares that the Jews are "the apple of His eye" (Zechariah 2:8; Deuteronomy 32:10; Psalm 17:8). *Apple* means the pupil or lens through which God views His creation. Don't poke a finger in God's eye by harming His chosen people! **Psalm 83** dramatizes the attack against Israel that we see being played out in the Middle East today. Israel's enemies are God's enemies. "Do not keep silent, O God! Do not hold **Your** peace, and do not be still, O God! For behold, **Your** enemies make a tumult; and those who hate **You** have lifted up their head. They have taken crafty counsel against **Your** people … They have said, 'Come, and let us cut them off from being a nation, that the name of **Israel** may be remembered no more" (vv. 1-4). Sound familiar? The Palestinian terrorists say

---

62 Bennett, p. 82.

they will drive Israel into the sea! The nations plotting against Israel in Psalm 83 are the same nations today, with modern names. God wants all the nations of the world to know that He is real, and He is showing Himself in the Middle East conflict today. Remember the story of the dry bones in Ezekiel? Many a preacher, seeking to revive a dead church, has begun his sermon with, "Can these bones live?" But these bones are identified **literally** in the vision to Ezekiel as "the whole house of Israel" (Ezekiel 37:11). We have to be careful about spiritualizing something that is obviously a prophecy concerning the nation Israel. Israel is God's timepiece, and if you pay attention, you can interpret the signs of the times prophesied in Scripture!

Norma Archbold, in her book, *The Mountains of Israel*, tells of the similarity of Middle East events with Chapters 35 and 36 of Ezekiel: "These chapters are two halves of a whole. Chapter 35 is a prophecy 'against' a mountain (Mount Seir), and Chapter 36 is a prophecy 'to' mountains (the mountains of Israel). Mount Seir and the mountains of Israel are the homelands of twin brothers Esau and Jacob, ancestors of today's Arabs and Jews. Although Chapter 35 contains warnings and Chapter 36 contains promises, the purpose is the same. Both chapters end with the same words, 'Then they shall know that I am the Lord.'" [63]

The "mountains" of Israel, are its heartland, Judea and Samaria. The world calls it the "West Bank." It was in this area where Abraham first came into Canaan and built an altar. Here on the mountain east of Bethel for the first time Abram called on the name of the Lord, YHWH. "On a satellite map over Israel you can see the sacred Name YHWH written in the mountain formations around Bethel with huge Hebrew letters! Today Islam is trying, with the help of the international community, to extinguish the Name of God from this place by creating a Palestinian Muslim state in this very area. It will never succeed!" [64]

---

63 Norma Parrish Archbold, *The Mountains of Israel, The Bible & the West Bank* (Phoebe's Song – Israel and USA, 1993, 1995, 1996), pp. vii-viii.
64 Lars Enarson, "Weekly Torah – Parashat Lech Lecha (Go) Commentary," www.thewatchman.org.

The best way for Christians to connect with their Jewish roots is to take a trip to Israel and walk where Jesus walked. My husband Curtis and I first went in 1994. Our Palestinian guide Simon pointed out fulfillment of Scripture, saying "The best thing that has happened to this land was when the Jews returned." Yes, the Holy Land was barren and in ruins until the Jews started coming back in the late 1800s. "And the desert shall rejoice and blossom as the rose. ... And the ransomed of the Lord shall return and come to Zion with singing, with everlasting joy on their heads ..." (Isa. 35:1, 10). It was at that time that Arabs began moving into Palestine to get jobs. Simon knew that he and his fellow Arabs were prospering because of the Jews. Indeed, the whole world has been blessed by the Jews as God promised Abraham: "I will make you a great nation; I will bless you and make your name great; and **you shall be a blessing**" (Genesis 12:2). My Master's thesis was about all the blessings the Jews have brought to the world. In the back of my book I included an Appendix from the thesis, "Blessings to the Nations by Individual Jews & the Nation of Israel,"[65] which is quite an impressive heritage!

A love of our Jewish roots will lead to a study of the modern history of Israel in which Bible prophecy is continually being fulfilled. The rebirth of the State of Israel on May 14, 1948 is a fulfillment of Isaiah 66:8 – "Whoever heard of such a thing? Who has ever seen such things? Is a country born in one day?" (CJB)

More prophetic Scriptures are being fulfilled in the increase of aliyah (Jewish immigration, "going up" to Israel) in our day. I have a whole chapter on this in my book.[66] After Israel was reborn in 1948, there was an airlift of 48,000 Jews from Yemen called "Operation Magic Carpet." The people believed God's promise, "...they shall mount up with wings as eagles." By 1950, Yemen was empty of Jews! Another outstanding instance of mass aliyah was Operation Solomon on May 24, 1991. In just 36 hours, 14,200 Ethiopians were airlifted from Addis Ababa to Israel! In his book,

---

65 Petrey, pp. 255-260.
66 Petrey, "In Whose Heart are the Highways to Zion," pp. 91-100.

37

Let My People Go![67] Tom Hess lists 700 verses from Scripture where God promises the land of Canaan to His chosen people as an **everlasting** possession and encourages them to return. Surely this great number of verses shows you what is closest to God's heart. It should be close to our hearts also.

As stated before, the "feasts of the Lord" offer thrilling insights into *Yeshua's* first and second comings and also the pouring out of the Holy Spirit on Pentecost. An excellent source is the beautifully illustrated book, *The Feasts of the Lord*, by Kevin Howard and Marvin Rosenthal.[68] Gentile believers are not obligated to keep the feasts (Acts 15:22-29), but this is one way to "provoke the Jews to jealousy" and also to see *Yeshua* hidden away in each feast, either already fulfilled or about to be! It is a growing trend for Christians to celebrate the Passover Seder and see the rich symbolism. After all, Jesus inaugurated the New Covenant at a Passover meal, which is celebrated in churches today in an abbreviated form as The Last Supper.

After His resurrection *Yeshua* was walking on the road to Emmaus with two of his followers and saw how discouraged they were because of His death. They did not recognize Him. "He said to them, 'O foolish ones, and slow of heart to believe in all that the prophets have spoken! Ought not the Messiah to have suffered these things and to enter into His glory?' And **beginning at Moses and all the Prophets**, He expounded to them in **all the Scriptures** the things concerning Himself." *Yeshua* taught them from Genesis throughout the Prophets, the whole Old Testament! Finally, their eyes were opened to see the risen Lord! "And they said to one another, 'Did not our heart burn within us while He talked with us on the road, and while **He opened the Scriptures to us?**" (Luke 24:25-27, 32)

Most definitely, Christians caring about their Jewish roots illuminates Scripture. Eyes are opened to see, and hearts burn with

---

67 Tom Hess, *Let My People Go!* (Jerusalem: Progressive Vision International, 1997).

68 Kevin Howard & Marvin Rosenthal, *The Feasts of the Lord* (Orlando: Zion's Hope, Inc., 1997).

fresh fire. "We will understand God's Word and be able to discern the prophetic times and seasons in which we are living."[69] This is because as grafted-in wild branches, we have become "a partaker of the root and richness of the olive tree" (Romans 11:17).

And may I suggest that when Christians truly care, they will do three things – PRAY, GIVE, AND GO! Every Christian should make at least one trip to Israel in his or her lifetime. I have been there seven times. It is a life-changing experience! According to Romans 15:27, we should give materially to ministries in Israel, especially to those who are actively evangelizing the Jewish people (as well as Arabs). But prayer undergirds everything we do, as we remember to "pray for the peace of Jerusalem" (Psalm 122:6). One day our Lord will return and rule the whole earth from His throne in Jerusalem! We should value our Jewish roots and **care about the Jewish people and Israel. It is all a part of our preparation as the Bride of a Jewish Messiah.** Come quickly, Lord *Yeshua*!

---

69 Richard Booker, *The Root and Branches, An Introduction to the Jewish Roots of Christianity* (The Woodlands, Texas: Sounds of the Trumpet, 2001), p. 9.